NOËL! 3

CAROLS AND ANTHEMS
FOR ADVENT, CHRISTMAS & EPIPHANY
FOR MIXED VOICE CHOIRS

T0039830

NOËL! 3

CAROLS AND ANTHEMS
FOR ADVENT, CHRISTMAS & EPIPHANY
FOR MIXED VOICE CHOIRS

Selected & edited by David Hill

NOVELLO

Introduction

The forty-five carols in *Noël! 3* have been chosen to reflect the increasing demands for new carols – and new arrangements of old favourites – by both sacred and secular choirs today. From the earliest carols to the present day, Christmas and its surrounding seasons have always been a time of inspiration and celebration: this volume provides an eclectic and exciting range of pieces from the Baroque to the contemporary, from the simplest of works to the more challenging.

Well-loved Christmas favourites have been included in new arrangements (*I wonder as I wander*; *Ding, dong! Merrily on high*; *Lo, how a rose e'er blooming*; *Tomorrow shall be my dancing day* and many more) alongside traditional folk tunes (*Hereford Carol*; *Quelle est cette odeur agréable*; *This is the truth sent from above*; and *Wexford Carol*) and both well- and lesser-known carols from earlier periods (including Hieronymus Praetorius's sparkling *Joseph lieber, Joseph mein*; Gaspar Fernandes's beautiful setting of an Aztec lullaby, *Xicochi*; and Adolphe Adam's timeless classic, *O holy night!*).

Each year sees an encouragingly large number of new carols performed by choirs around the world. We have reflected this in our choices, and offer some of the very best contemporary carols, both from established composers (including Paul Mealor, Richard Allain, John Tavener, Richard Rodney Bennett and Francis Pott) and lesser-known contributors. Several pieces (*Lute-Book Lullaby*; *Lullay my liking*; *The Burning Babe*; and *My Jesu, sleep*) have been written specially for this volume. Two of the carols, *In the Snow* and *The holly and the ivy*, were winners of *The Times* 2011 carol competition.

We have endeavoured to provide a balance between fast and slow carols – singable examples of the former have not always been easy to find – and have worked to ensure that the collection is accessible to both amateur and professional singers. In addition, we have included a number of secular works (*Deck the hall*; *In the Snow*; *Walking in the Air*; and *We wish you a merry Christmas*) that we hope choirs of all types will find enjoyable.

I am enormously grateful to my colleagues at Novello for their input, advice and expertise; in particular to Jonathan Wikeley, Daniel Rollison, Matthew Berry, Kate Johnson, Chris Hinkins and Howard Friend. Many other people contributed to the production of this book and I would particularly like to thank John Hughes, Andrew Nethsingha, Ben Nicholas, Christopher Robinson, Stuart Nicholson, Christopher Johns, Geoffrey Webber and Matthew Owens.

David Hill
Cambridge, June 2012

Contents

FRONT COVER *Nativity* (c.1913-14, painted limestone) by Eric Gill (1882-1940)
by kind permission of The Eric Gill Estate and the Bridgeman Art Library

BACK COVER photograph of David Hill by Paul Troughton

MUSIC SETTING Chris Hinkins
PROJECT MANAGEMENT Jonathan Wikeley

Order No. NOV310838
ISBN 978-1-78038-600-3

© Copyright 2012 Novello & Company Limited.
Published in Great Britain by Novello Publishing Limited.

HEAD OFFICE
14-15 Berners Street,
London W1T 3LJ
UK
Tel. +44 (0)20 7434 0066
Fax +44 (0)20 7287 6329

SALES AND HIRE
Music Sales Distribution Centre,
Newmarket Road,
Bury St Edmunds,
Suffolk IP33 3YB
UK
Tel. +44 (0)1284 702600
Fax +44 (0)1284 768301

www.musicsales.com
e-mail: music@musicsales.co.uk

for Ellie

A Lullaby of the Nativity

Anon. (15th century)

Richard Blackford

Lul - lay, my lik - ing, my dere son, my sweet - ing,__ Lul - lay, my dere heart, my own dere dar - ling.

1. I saw a fair maid - en sit - ten and sing, She lulled a lit - tle

2

dere heart, my own dere dar-ling.

mf unis.

p

2.Ther was me-kil me-lo-dy at that child-es

T.
B.

birth, Al-le tho wern in hev-ne blis they ma-de me-kil mirth.

S.
A.

unis. f

3. An-gels bright, they sung that night and sei-den to that child, 'Bless-ed be thou and

T.
B.

unis.

(f)

ff

To the memory of a wonderful lady, Audrey Halliwell,
& to all my friends in the University of Aberdeen Chamber Choir

A spotless rose
No. 4 from Now Sleeps the Crimson Petal

Anon. (16th century)
Trans. Catherine Winkworth

Paul Mealor

* Bracketed notes are optional divisi.

9

10

12

for the Musicians Benevolent Fund

Annunciation

From the Gospel
according to St Luke

John Tavener

*Soloists are preferred, but a semichorus may be substituted if necessary.
** 'Oh' as in the 'o' of log'. Breathe when necessary but not simultaneously.

14

16

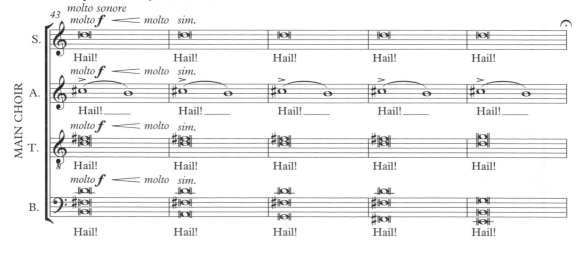

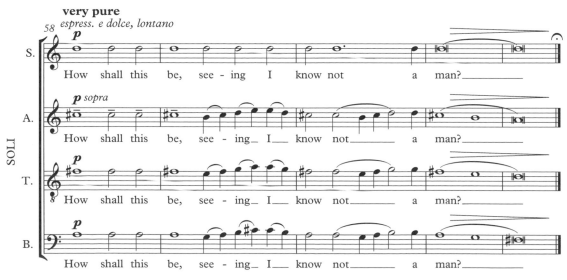

N'aldretts, Sunday of the Cross
29 March 1992

As I lay upon a night

Alma redemptoris mater

Middle English poem

Jamie W. Hall

'Hail be thou bliss - ful wight,___ to ben clep'd now___ art though dight', Re - demp - - - to - ris ma - ter.

Più mosso, con moto
Freely
TENOR SOLO

At that word that la - - dy bright a - non con - ceiv - ed God___ full___ of might; Then men___ wist well that she___ hight. Re - demp - - to - ris ma - ter.

Poco più mosso

ah___

When Je - su on___ the rood was pight, Ma - ry was dole - ful of that

sub. meno mosso

till she see him rise up-right, Re - demp - to-ris ma - ter.

sight

Je - su that sit-test in hea-ven light, Grant us to co-men be-forn thy

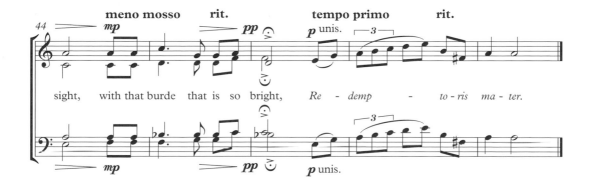

meno mosso **rit.** **tempo primo** **rit.**

sight, with that burde that is so bright, Re - demp - to-ris ma - ter.

burd – maiden   anon – straight away
clep'n – call   wist – knew
wight – person   hight – named
clep'd – called   rood – cross
dight – appointed   pight – pitched

for A.M.B.

Balulalow

Wedderburn

Richard Allain

24

Norwich/London, 1983

to Jilly

Balulalow

Wedderburn

James Burton

Benedicamus Domino

Sloane MS. 2593 (15th century)

Peter Warlock

30

With the boy-child's coming forth
Joy! For us the promised time!
Coming forth from the virgin's womb
Glory and praise be!
God made man and yet undying.

Not of human generation
He is born of a virgin:
Not of human machination
He is born of Mary:
In this endless holy day
We do bless the Lord!

for Mark Williams and the Choirs of Jesus College, Cambridge

Bright Star Carol

Robert Herrick

Nico Muhly

38

*Slowly change vowel, singer by singer, between an 'oh' and an 'ee' sound. Random, calm shifts.

40

*When a 'Z' appears on a stem in the vocal parts each singer should repeat
the text freely on the given pitches, in any tempo, being careful not to co-ordinate
precisely with other singers. One's individual rate of text chanting can and should change
throughout these sections. The text repeats until a new text is given.

for Scott Farrell and the choir of the Cathedral Church of St. Nicholas, Newcastle upon Tyne

Child of the stable's secret birth

Timothy Dudley-Smith

Samuel Rathbone

Verse 1: SOPRANOS & ALTOS
Verse 2: TENORS & BASSES *p*

1. Child of the sta - ble's_ se - cret birth, The Lord by
2. Eyes_ that shine_ in the lan - tern's ray, A face so

right of the lords_ of_ earth,_ Let an - gels_ sing of a king_ new born, The
small in its nest_ of_ hay,_ Face_ of a child who is born_ to scan The

3. Voice that rang through the courts on high,

Con-trac-ted now to a

A voice to mas-ter the wind and wave, The hu-man
word-less cry,

heart and the hun-gry grave: The voice of God through the ce-dar

trees,___ Roll - ing forth as the sound of the seas.__

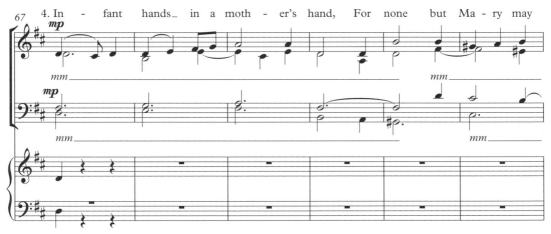

4. In - fant hands_ in a moth - er's hand, For none but Ma - ry may

un - der - stand_ Whose are___ the_ hands and the fing - ers curled But

his___ who fash-ioned and made_ our world;

And through__ these_ hands_ in the

hour_ of death____ Nails_ shall strike to the wood____ be - neath._

allargando   a tempo
unis. *mf*
5.Child of the sta - ble's_

se - cret birth, The Fath - er's gift to a way - ward_ earth,_ To drain__ the_

cup in a few short years Of all our sor-rows, our sins and

Ours is the prize

tears, Ours is the prize for the road he trod, Ris'n with

Christ, at peace with God.

+32'   *29 October 2003*

Commissioned and first performed by YiRu Hall and the Portsmouth Grammar School Chamber Choir
at Portsmouth Cathedral on 14 December 2011

to Margaret and George Rizza

Coventry Carol

Anon. (16th century)

Richard Rodney Bennett

Char - gèd he hath this___ day,_____ His men of

Char - gèd he hath this day,_____ His men of___

Char - gèd he hath this___ day,_____ His men of

Char - gèd he hath this___ day,_____ His men of

might in his own___ sight, All young___ child - ren to slay.___

might in his own___ sight, All young child - ren to slay.___

might in his own___ sight, All young___ child - ren to slay.___

might in his own___ sight, All young child - ren to slay.___

56

lay. Lul - ly,_____ lul - la, thou lit - tle ti - ny
lay. Lul - ly,_____ lul - la, thou lit - tle ti - ny
lay. Lul - ly,_____ lul - la, thou lit - tle ti - ny
lay. Lul - ly,_____ lul - la, thou lit - tle

child,_____ By by,_____ lul - ly, lul - lay.
child,_____ By by,_____ lul - ly, lul - lay.
child,_____ By by,_____ lul - ly, lul - lay.
child,_____ By by,_____ lul - ly, lul - lay.

London
31 December 2010

Deck the hall with boughs of holly

Anon. (19th century)

Trad. Welsh
arr. Adrian Lucas

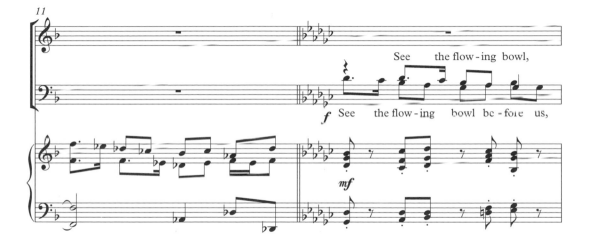

Fast a-way the old year pass - es, *fa la la la la la la la la*

Hail the new, ye lads and lass - es, *fa la la la la la la la la*

Laugh-ing, quaff-ing al - to-ge - ther, *fa la la la la la la la la la la la*

62

Ding dong! Merrily on high

G. R. Woodward

French tune
arr. Malcolm Williamson

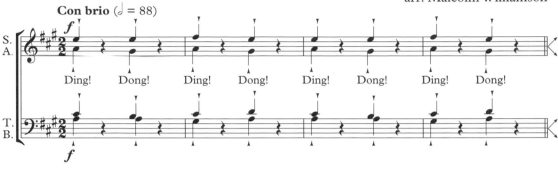

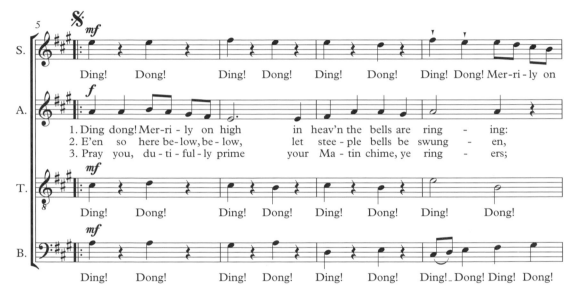

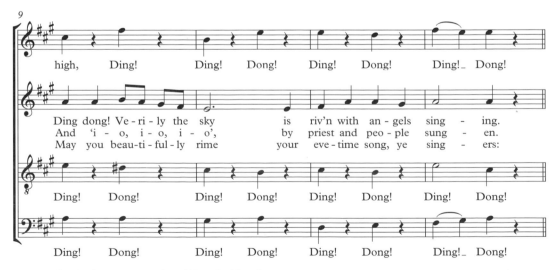

The A. line in the verses can be stiffened with a S. or two.
The punctuating S.T.B. chords must be rhythmically precise.
The A. tune should be carefully shaped. S. must avoid a lumpy four-in-the-bar feeling in the refrain.

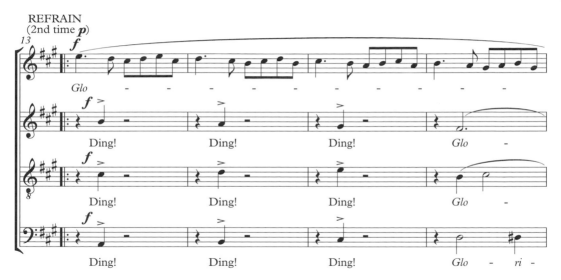

Hereford Carol

Trad. Herefordshire
arr. Christopher Robinson

68

all our praise_ be; May__ we fol-low and

all our praise_ be; May__ we his__ steps then fol - low and_

he our pat-tern be; So when our lives_ are_ end - ed, we all may hear him

he our_ pat-tern be; So when our lives_ are_ end - ed, we all may hear him

poco rit.

call: 'Come, souls, re-ceive the king - dom pre - pared for you all.'

call: 'Come,_ souls, re - ceive the king - dom pre - pared_ for you_ all.'

poco rit.

Hodie Christus natus est

No. 3 from *Three Christmas Motets*

Magnificat antiphon,
Christmas Day Vespers

Dan Locklair

76

78

30 July 1993
Winston-Salem, NC

For the wedding of Julia Hughes and Michał Hul, Tudeley, Kent

Hurry on to Bethlehem

Trad. Polish
arr. Jonathan Wikeley

82

85

to Kate Johnson

I Saw Three Ships

Anon.

Richard Rodney Bennett

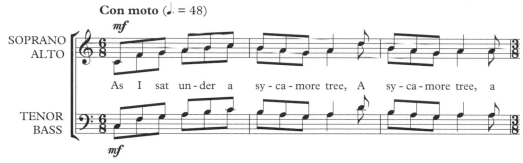

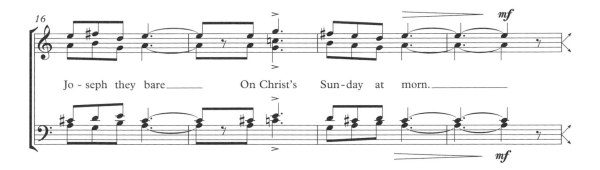

Jo - seph they bare_____ On Christ's Sun-day at morn._____

S. Jo - seph did whis-tle and Ma-ry did sing, Ma - ry did sing, Ma - ry did sing.___

A. Jo - seph did whis-tle and Ma-ry did sing, Ma - ry did sing.___

T. Jo - seph did whis - tle, Ma - ry did___ sing.___

B. Jo - seph did whis - tle, Ma - ry did sing.___

(Piano reduction for rehearsal only)

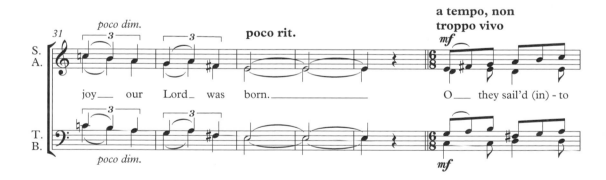

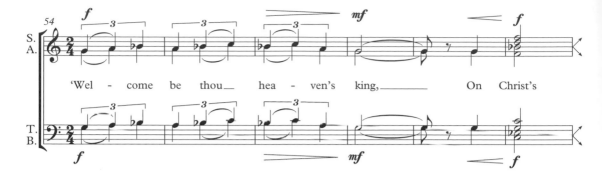

'Wel - come be thou___ hea - ven's king,_____ On Christ's

poco a poco largamente

Sun - day,___ On Christ's Sun - day_____ at morn.'

Sun - day,___ On Christ's Sun - day_____ at morn.'

Sun - day,___ On Christ's Sun - day_____ at morn.'

Sun - day,___ On Christ's Sun - day_____ at morn.'

I wonder as I wander

John Jacob Niles

John Jacob Niles
arr. Matthew O'Donovan

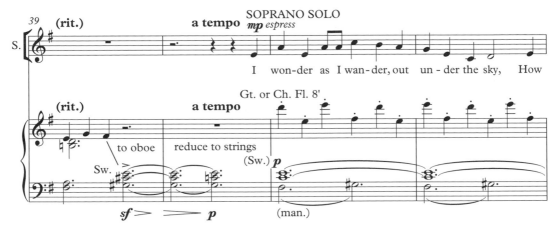

I won-der as I wan-der, out un-der the sky, How

Je-sus the sa-viour did come for to die, For poor orn-'ry peo-ple like you and like I... I

won-der as I wan-der,_____ out un-der the sky.

For Stephen Cleobury and the Choir of King's College, Cambridge

In the bleak mid-winter

Christina Rossetti

Richard Allain

96

Norwich, 20 July 2011

Joint winner of The Times Carol Competition 2011

In the Snow

Words and music:
Pippa Cleary

Soprano 2, Tenor and Bass solos may all be sung by a semichorus.

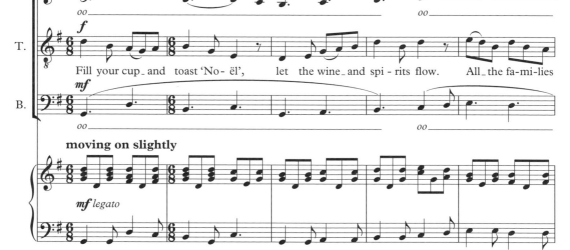

SOPRANO 2 SOLO

mf

Look at the world and see it glit-ter, hid-den be-neath a bed of white.

Ev-'ry-thing spark-les and ev-'ry-thing glows, danc-ing and sing-ing in the snow.

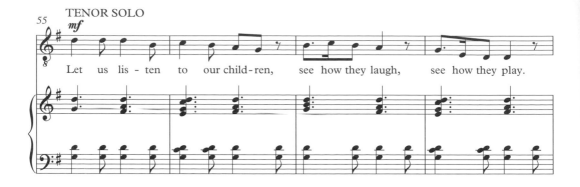

TENOR SOLO

mf

Let us lis - ten to our child-ren, see how they laugh, see how they play.

Com-ing to-ge-ther all ov - er the world,_ danc-ing and sing - ing in_ the snow.

SOPRANO 1 SOLO

f

So_ let our hearts be filled_ with glad - ness_____ Just_ as the

SOPRANO 2 ONLY

mp

FULL

mp

S.

oo_____ oo_____

A.

mp

oo_____ oo_____

(FULL TENORS)

mp

T.

oo_____

f

*Optional riff in the musical theatre style.

*Optional riff in the musical theatre style.

*Optional riff in the musical theatre style.

112

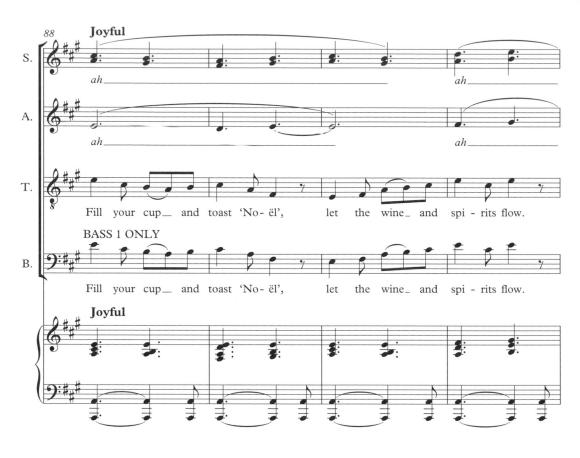

113

Joseph and the Angel

Words and music:
R. R. Terry

to Keith Miller-Jones

In Wintertime

Betty Askwith

Lennox Berkeley Op. 103

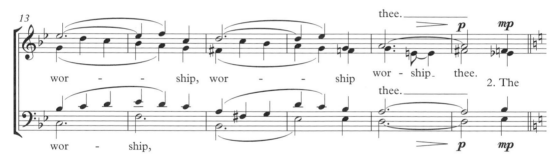

* Optional for organ.

To Andrew Dibb and the choir of Ranby House School, Christmas 2004

Infant holy, infant lowly

Trad. Polish
tr. Edith Reed

Keith Roberts

120

(Ped.)

Joseph lieber, Joseph mein

Cantiones Sacrae
Hamburg 1622

Hieronymus Praetorius

124

130

29

32

133

Lo, how a rose e'er blooming

Es ist ein Ros' entsprungen

German carol
tr. Theodore Baker

Michael Praetorius
arr. Jan Sandström

136

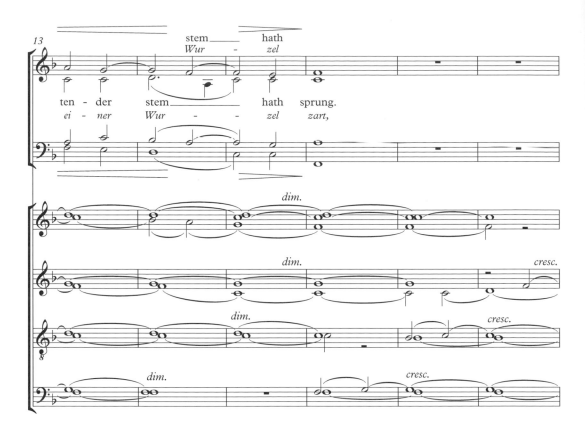

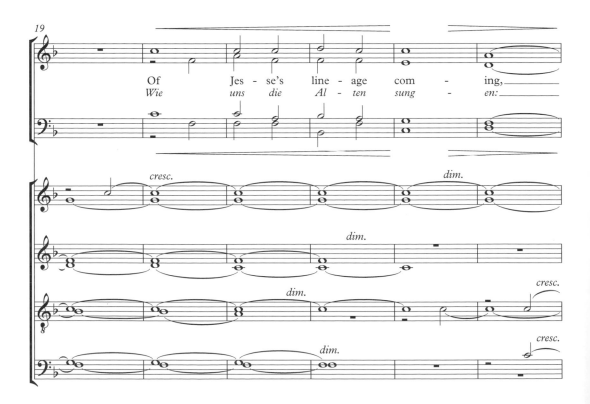

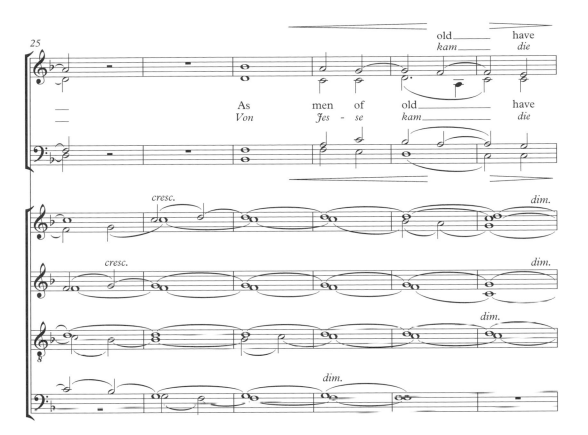

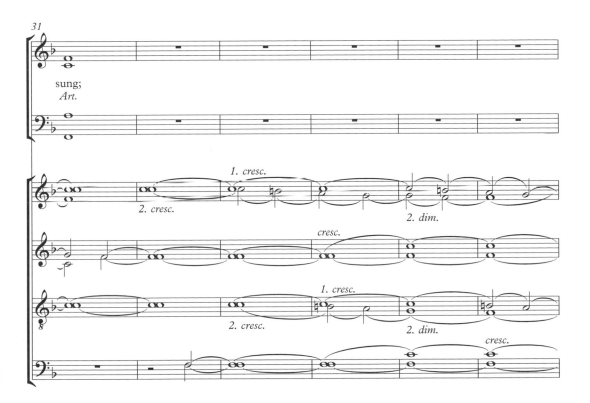

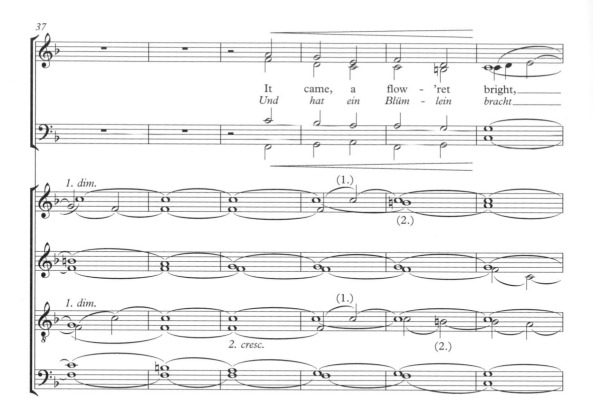

It came, a flow – 'ret bright,_____
Und hat ein Blüm – lein bracht_____

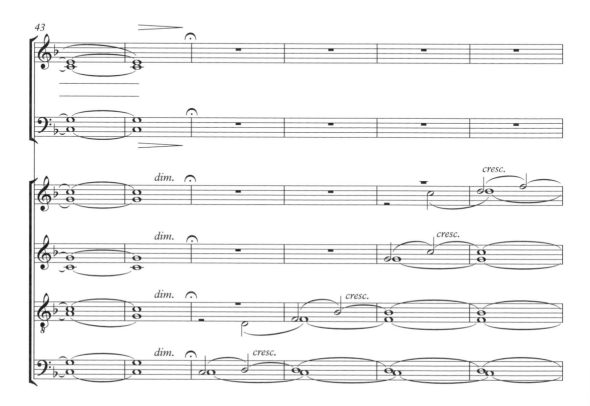

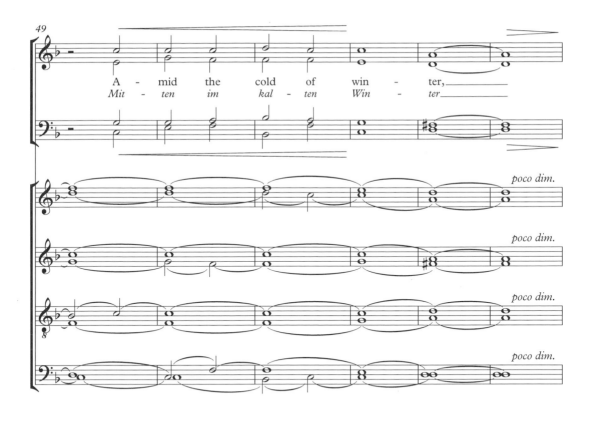

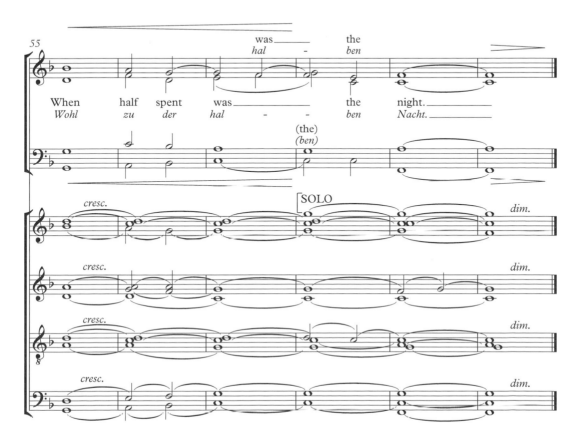

Lullay, my liking

Anon. (15th century)

David Hill

142

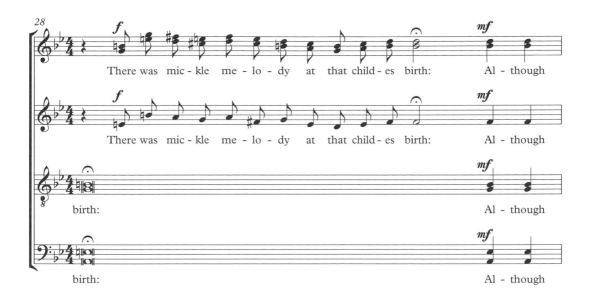

144

Lul-lay, my lik-ing, my dear son, my sweet-ing; Lul-lay, my dear heart, mine own dear

dar - ling. _____ (ng) _____

TENOR SOLO
strong, with joy

An - gels bright they sang that night, and

said-en to that child, 'Bless-ed be thou and so__ be she, that is so meek__ and mild'.

43 grant them all his bless - ing, that now_ mak - en cheer.

grant them all his bless - ing, that now_ mak - en cheer.

gradually open to 'ah' (ah)

gradually open to 'ah' (ah)

gradually open to 'ah' (ah)

gradually open to 'ah' (ah)

46 (S. SOLO) *mp calm*

Lul - lay, my lik - ing, my dear son, my sweet - ing,

S. *mm*

A. *mm*

Slower **poco rit.**

48 *p* (FULL) *ten.* *pp*

S. Lul - lay, my dear heart, mine own dear dar - ling.

A. Lul - lay, my dar - ling.

T. Lul - lay,_ my dar - ling.

B. Lul - lay, my dar - ling.

My Jesu, sleep

Rev. H. R. Bramley

Adam Harvey

Tenor solo / choir hum 'O lamb, my love inviting,
O star, my soul delighting,
O flower of mine own bearing,
O jewèl past comparing!
My darling, do not weep, my Jesu, sleep!'

Soprano solo / choir hum 'My child, of might indwelling,
My sweet, all sweets excelling,
Of bliss the fountain flowing,
The dayspring ever glowing!
My darling, do not weep, my Jesu, sleep!'

Full 'My joy, my exultation,
My spirit's consolation;
My son, my spouse, my brother,
O listen to thy mother!
My darling, do not weep, my Jesu, sleep!'

For Matthew Berry and Commotio,
in admiration and gratitude

Lute-Book Lullaby

Text from the Lute-Book of
William Ballet (17th century)

Francis Pott

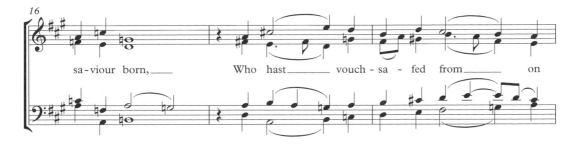

sa-viour born,_____ Who hast_____ vouch-sa-fed from_____ on

poco movendo

high_____ To_ vi-sit us_____ that were for-lorn. Lul-la-by,_____

poco ritard.

la-lu-la, lul-la-by._____ Sweet babe',_____

pochino meno mosso

sang__ she, And rock'd him sweet-ly on__ her knee,_____ and rock'd him

calando

sweet-ly on_____ her_ knee.

on_____ her_ knee.

Littleton, Winchester,
7 February 2012

Mary, that mother mild

Kölner Gesangbuch 1623
trans. Rev. George R. Woodward

Kölner Gesangbuch 1623
arr. Adrian Lucas

10

there   Babe Je - sus needs must bear;   And   there, at God's com -
bright,   And Is - ra - el's de - light.   A   pro - phet-ess then

there   Babe_ Je - sus needs must bear;   And   there, at God's com -
bright,_____   And_ Is - ra - el's de - light.   A   pro - phet-ess then_

there_____   Babe_ Je - sus_ needs must_ bear;   And   there, at God's com -
bright,_____   And_ Is - ra - el's de - light.   A   pro - phet-ess then_

there_____   Babe Je - sus needs must bear;   And   there, at God's com -
bright,_____   And_ Is - ra - el's de - light.   A__ pro - phet-ess then

14

- mand,   Good Si - me - on did   stand: The
came,   And An - na was her   name: Of

- mand,_ Good Si - me - on_____ did_____ stand:_ The old_ man
came,_ And An - na_ was_____ her_____ name:_ Of Ma - ry's

- mand, Good_ Si - - - me - on__ did   stand: The_ old_ man
came,   And An - - - na_ was her   name: Of_ Ma - ry's

- mand, Good_ Si - me - on did_____   stand:_____ The_
came,   And_ An - na_ was her_____   name:_____ Of_

17

old man fond - ly pressed   The in - fant to his breast,   The
Ma - ry's gen - tle boy,   Spake she with ho - ly joy;   E'en

fond - ly pressed   The in - fant to his breast,   The
gen - tle boy,   Spake she with ho - ly joy;   E'en

fond - ly pressed   The in - fant to his breast,   The
gen - tle boy,   Spake she with ho - ly joy;   E'en

old man fond - ly pressed The in - fant to his breast,   The
Ma - ry's gen - tle boy, Spake she with ho - ly joy;   E'en

21

Christ ex - pec - ted long,   The bur - then of his song.
so, Christ-child, draw near,   Our souls in such wise cheer.

Christ ex - pec - ted long, The bur - then of his song.
so, Christ-child, draw near, Our souls in such wise cheer.

Christ ex - pec - ted long, The bur - then of his song.
so, Christ-child, draw near, Our souls in such wise cheer.

Christ ex - pec - ted long, The bur - then of his song.
so, Christ-child, draw near, Our souls in such wise cheer.

O holy night!
("Noël")

Placide Cappeau
trans. J. S. Dwight

Adolphe Adam
arr. John E. West

O ho - ly night!_ the stars are bright-ly

shin - ing, It is the night of the dear sa-viour's birth;

Long lay the world_ in sin and er - ror pin - ing, Till he ap-

154

156

160

162

In celebration of Baby G

O magnum mysterium

No. 2 from *Three Christmas Motets*

Fourth responsory,
Christmas Day Matins

Dan Locklair

13-14 July 1993

O mortal man
(Sussex Mummers' Carol)

Trad. Sussex carol

arr. Herbert Howells
ed. Christopher Palmer

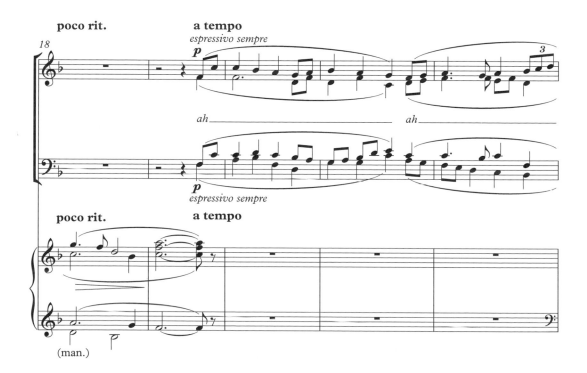

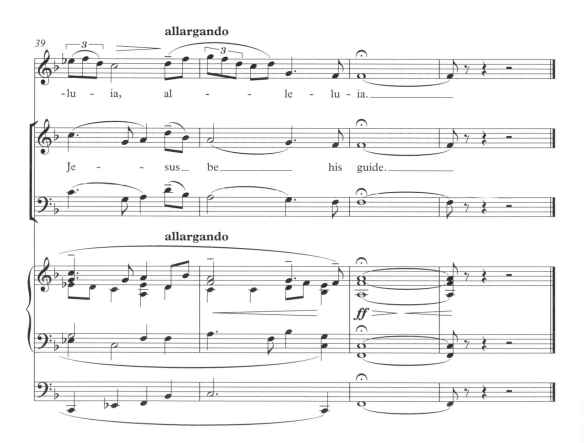

for Arianna

The Burning Babe

Robert Southwell

Jonathan Wikeley

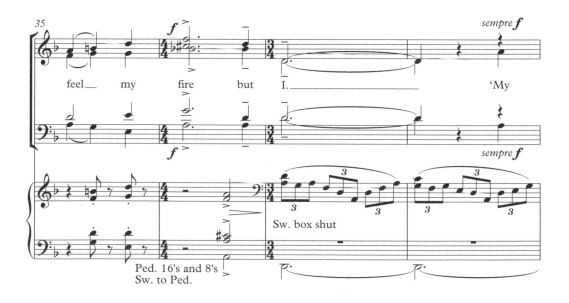

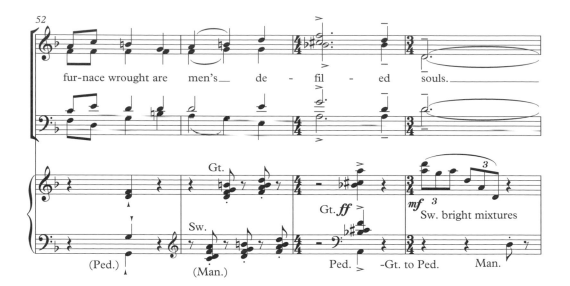

fur-nace wrought are men's___ de - fil - ed souls.___

Gt.

Sw.

(Ped.) (Man.) Ped. -Gt. to Ped. Man.

Gt. *ff*

mf 3 Sw. bright mixtures

unis. *ff*

For which, as now on fire I am to work them to their

unis.

ff

good, So I will melt in - to a bath to wash them in my

Dedicated to the Choir of St Columba's Church, Maryhill, Glasgow

O Radiant Dawn

Antiphon for 21st December

James MacMillan

* Grace notes always on the the beat.

Quelle est cette odeur agréable

Verse 1: Full *mp*
Verse 2: S1 solo with S2ATB humming *p*
Verse 5: Full *f*

Trad. French
arr. Matthew O'Donovan

Verse 3: First tenors sing melody *mf*, the rest sing *mp*.
Verse 4: Tenor solo *mp espress*, accompaniment *p*.

*Singers should stagger breathing throughout the verse.

Joint winner of The Times Carol Competition 2011

The holly and the ivy

Trad. English carol
(17th-18th century)

Stuart Thompson

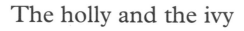

ORGAN

SOPRANOS & ALTOS *mf*

The hol - ly and the i - vy,____ When they are both full

grown, Of all the trees that are in the wood, The hol - ly bears the

crown: The ris - ing of the sun____ And the run - ning of the

deer, The play - ing of the mer - ry or-gan, Sweet sing-ing in the

choir.

S. The hol - ly bears a blos-som,___ As white as the li - ly

A. The hol - ly bears_ a blos - som, As white as the li - ly

T. The hol - ly bears a blos - som, As white as the li - ly

B. The hol - ly bears a blos - som, As white as the li - ly

deer, The play-ing of the mer-ry or-gan, Sweet sing-ing in the

deer,_ The play-ing of_ the mer-ry or-gan, Sweet sing - ing in_ the

deer,_ The play-ing of_ the mer-ry or-gan, Sweet sing - ing in_ the

deer, The play-ing of the mer-ry or-gan, Sweet sing-ing in the

choir.

choir. The

choir.

choir. The

188

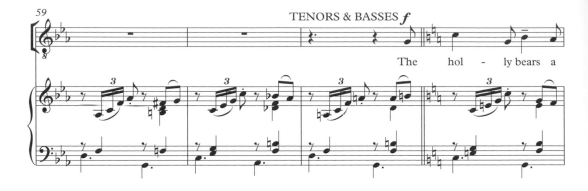

192

sing-ing in the choir.

sing - ing in the choir.

sing - ing in the choir.

sing-ing in the choir.

molto rall.

molto rall.

for Thomas Lydon & The Rhinegold Singers

There is no rose

Anon. (15th century)

Andrew Cusworth

194

8 November 2010

This is the truth sent from above

Trad. Herefordshire
collected and arr. Ralph Vaughan Williams

did ap - pear;_ He_ here did_ live,_ and_ here did preach,_ And_

ma - ny thou - sands_ he_ did teach.   Thus

FULL unis. *f*

mf *cresc.* *f*

Man. Ped.

he in love_ to_ us be - haved, To show us how_ we must be saved; And_

if you want to_ know the way, Be_ pleas'd to hear_ what_ he_ did say.

molto rall.
molto rall.

to Victoria

Tomorrow shall be my dancing day

Old Cornish poem

Trad. English
arr. Stuart Nicholson

To - mor-row shall be_ my dan - cing day, I would_ my true_ love

did_ so chance To_ see the le - gend of_ my play, To call my true_ love

208

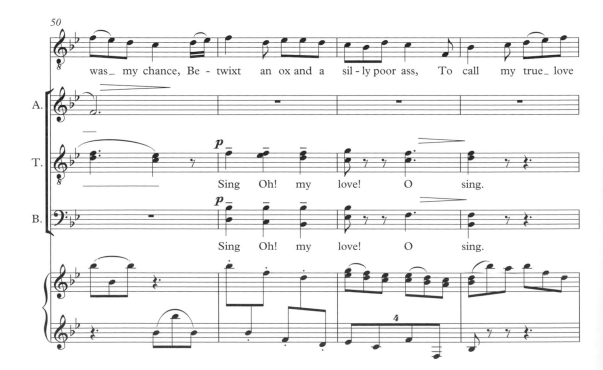

210

* Altos & basses may omit from bar 67, last beat, to the upbeat of bar 74.

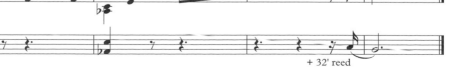

Tua Bethlem dref

Welsh carol

David Davies
arr. Geoffrey Webber

* Singers should stagger breathing in hummed or ah-ed sections
  (bars 1-12, 21-28, 30-37 and 46-end).

1. On to Bethlehem town;
   Join the crowd and travel down,
   Down the road that leads us to the cradle.
   Come all who are able.
   Come, come to the stable with
   Hearts full of joy as we kneel and pray.
   Come and see the child
   With his mother Mary mild.
   Come along and worship at the cradle.

2. There we'll see the boy;
   Hearts aglow with boundless joy;
   In the everlasting word.
   We will bow before him;
   Come, come and adore him,
   Bringing gifts of gold, frankincense and myrrh.
   On to Bethlehem town;
   Join the crowd and travel down,
   Down the road that leads us to the cradle.

Words in italics offer a phonetic pronunciation guide.
In addition, choirs should note the following pronunciations:

ch pronounced as in *loch*
th pronounced as in *thatch*
dd pronounced as in *this*
oun pronounced as in *noun*

'Twas in the winter cold

A Christmas morning hymn

Rev. C. J. Black

Joseph Barnby

Walking in the Air

Theme from 'The Snowman'

An arrangement of the song from the animated film
of 'The Snowman' for SATB chorus and piano

Lyrics by Howard Blake (1982)

Music by Howard Blake (1982)
This arrangement by Howard Blake Op. 624 (2011)

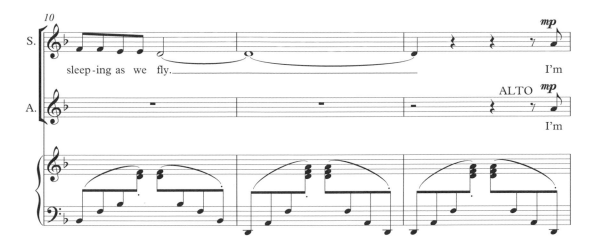

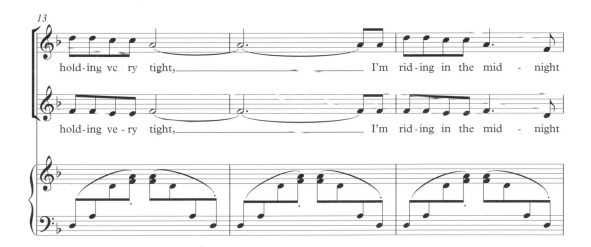

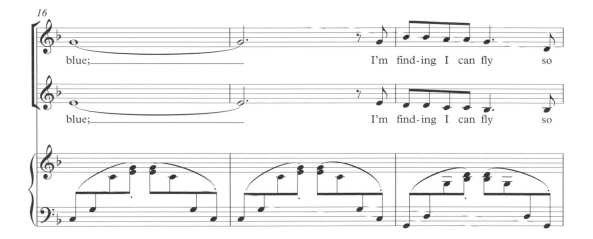

high a-bove with you.

high a-bove with you.

On a-cross the world ___ the

vil - la - ges go by   like dreams,_____   the

riv - ers and the hills,   the for - ests and the streams._____

Child - ren gaze   o - pen mouthed,   tak - en by   sur -

-prise; no-bo-dy down be-low be-

-lieves their eyes. We're surf-ing in the air,

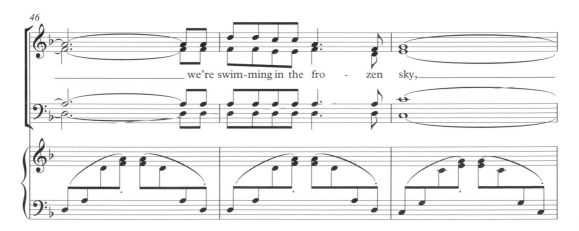

we're swim-ming in the fro - zen sky,

we're drift-ing ov - er i - cy moun-tains float-ing by.

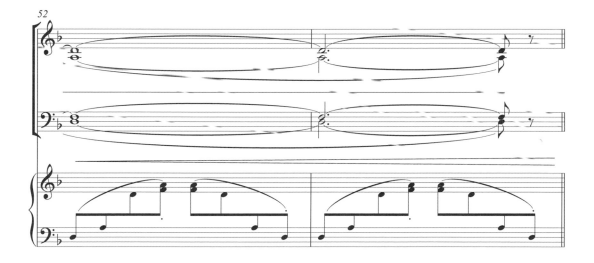

poco dim.

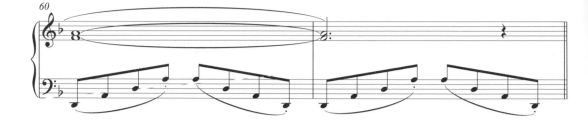

Sud-den-ly, swoop-ing low on an o - cean

deep, rous-ing up a might-y mon - ster

from_____ his__ sleep._____ We're

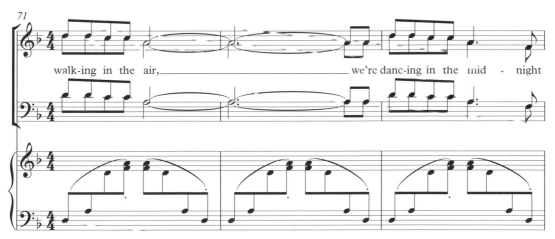

walk-ing in the air,_____ we're danc-ing in the mid - night

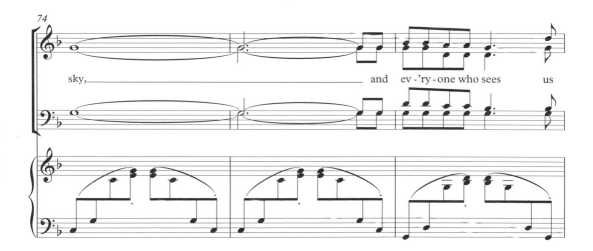

sky,_____ and ev -'ry - one who sees us

greets us as we fly._____ Walk-ing in the air,_____

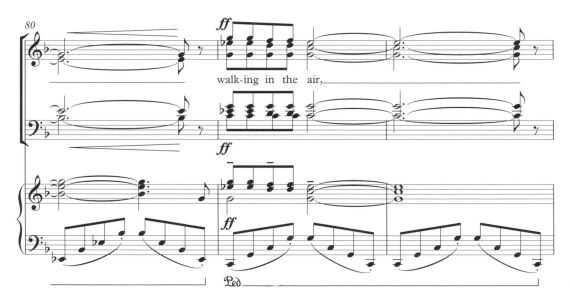

walk-ing in the air,_____

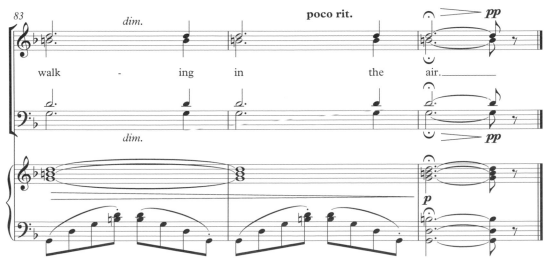

walk - ing in the air._____

We wish you a merry Christmas

West Country song
arr. John Gardner

To S.J.N.

Wexford Carol

Trad. Irish
arr. Timothy Noon

* Singers should gently restrike repeated notes in
hummed or ah-ed sections, as if on a harp or piano.

238

BARITONE SOLO *mf*

The night be - fore the hap-py tide The

no - ble vir - gin and her guide Were long time seek - ing up and down To

* Depending on the size of choir, this section can be sung to 'ah'.

242

To Alison

Winter's Wait

Robert Tear

James Whitbourn

8' only

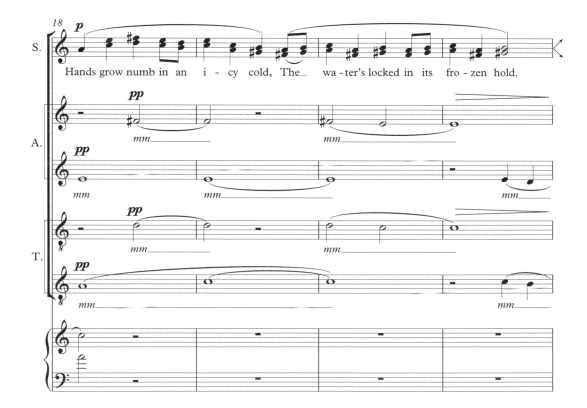

S. All wait for the sun, all wait.

A. wait, all wait.

T. wait, all wait.

B. wait, wait, all wait.

252

Xicochi

Aztec carol

Gaspar Fernandes

Gently sleep, little child. The angels rock your cradle. Alleluia.

Nahuatl pronunciation guide: Xicochi = *Shee - co - chee*
joco = *ho -* (aspirated h, *o* as in '*hot*') *coe*
caomiz = *cow - meez* angelos = *an - ghel - (hard g) os*

2 3 4 5 6 7 8 9